小马外语

扫描二维码
收听全书音频

中英对照彩绘珍藏版

飞鸟集

泰戈尔作品集

（印）泰戈尔（Tagore） 著
郑振铎 译

化学工业出版社
·北京·

一九二二年版《飞鸟集》例言

　　译诗是一件最不容易的工作。 原诗音节的保留固然是绝不可能的事！就是原诗意义的完全移植，也有十分的困难。 散文诗算是最容易译的，但有时也须费十分的力气。 如惠德曼（Walt Whitman）的《草叶集》便是一个例子。 这有两个原因：第一，有许多诗中特用的美丽文句，差不多是不能移动的。 在一种文字里，这种字眼是"诗的"、是"美的"，如果把它移植在第二种文字中，不是找不到相当的好字，便是把原意丑化了，变成非"诗的"了。 在泰戈尔的《人格论》中，曾讨论到这一层。 他以为诗总是要选择那"有生气的"字眼，——就是那些不仅仅为报告用而能融化于我们心中，不因市井常用而损坏它的形式的字眼。 譬如在英文里，"意识"（consciousness）这个词，带有多少科学的意义，所以诗中不常用它。 印度文的"同意"（chetana）则是一个"有生气"而常用于诗歌里的词。 又如英文的"感情"（feeling）这个字是充满了生命的，但彭加

利文 ① 里的"同意"（anubhuti）则诗中绝无用之者。在这些地方，译诗的人实在感到万分的困难。第二，诗歌的文句总是含蓄的、暗示的。它的句法的构造，多简短而含义丰富。有的时候，简直不能译。如直译，则不能达意。如稍加诠释，则又把原文的风韵与含蓄完全消灭，而使之不成一首诗了。

因此，我主张诗集的介绍，只应当在可能的范围选择，而不能——也不必——完全整册地搬运过来。

大概诗歌的选译，有两个方便的地方：第一，选择可以适应译者的兴趣。在一本诗集中的许多诗，译者未必都十分喜欢它。如果不十分喜欢它，不十分感觉得它的美好，则他的译文必不能十分得神，至少也把这快乐的工作变成一种无意义的苦役。选译则可以减灭译者的这层痛苦。第二，便是减少上述的两层翻译上的困难。因为如此便可以把不能译的诗，不必译出来。译出来而丑化了或是为读者所看不懂，则反不如不译的好。

但我并不是在这里宣传选译主义。诗集的全选，是我所极端希望而且欢迎的。不过这种工作应当让给那些有全译能力的译者去做。我为自己的兴趣与能力所限制，实在不敢担任这种重大的工作。且为大多数的译者计，我也主张选译是较好的一种译诗方法。

现在我译泰戈尔的诗，便实行了这种选译的主张，以前我

也有全译泰戈尔各诗集的野心。有好些友人也极力劝我把它们全译出来。我试了几次。但我的野心与被大家鼓起的勇气，终于给我的能力与兴趣打败了。

现在所译的泰戈尔各集的诗，都是我所最喜欢读的，而且是我的能力所比较的能够译得出的。

有许多诗，我自信是能够译得出的，但因为自己翻译它们的兴趣不大强烈，便不高兴去译它们。还有许多诗我是很喜欢读它们，而且是极愿意把它们译出来的。但因为自己能力的不允许，便也只好舍弃了它们。

即在这些译出的诗中，有许多也是自己觉得译得不好，心中很不满意的。但实在不忍再割舍它们了。只好请读者赏读它的原意，不必注意于粗陋的译文。

泰戈尔的诗集用英文出版的共有以下六部。

（一）《园丁集》（*The Gardener*）
（二）《吉檀迦利》（*Gitanjali*）
（三）《新月集》（*The Crescent Moon*）
（四）《采果集》（*Fruit-Gathering*）
（五）《飞鸟集》（*Stray Birds*）
（六）《爱者之贻与歧路》（*Lover's Gift and Grossing*）

但据 B.K.Roy 的《泰戈尔与其诗》（*R.Tagore The Man and His Poetry*）一书上所载，他用彭加利文写的重要诗集，却有下面的许多种。

Sandhva Sangit、Kshanika,

Probhat Sangit、Kanika,

Bhanusingher Padabali、Kahini,

Chabi O Gan、Sishn、

Kari O Komal、Naibadya,

Prakritir Pratisodh、Utsharga,

Sonartari、Kheya、

Chaitali、Gitanzali、

Kalpana、Gitimalya,

Katha.

　　我的这几本诗选，是根据那六部用英文写的诗集译下来的。因为我不懂梵文。

　　在这几部诗集中，间有重出的诗篇，如《海边》一诗，已见于《新月集》中，而又列入《吉檀迦利》，排为第六十首。《飞鸟集》的第九十八首，也与同集中的第二百六十三首相同。像这一类的诗篇，都照先见之例，把它列入最初见的地方。

　　我的译文自信是很忠实的。误解的地方，却也保不定完全没有。如读者偶有发现，肯公开地指教我，那是我所异常欢迎的。

郑振铎

一九二二、六、二六

一九三三年版本序

《飞鸟集》曾经全译出来一次，因为我自己的不满意，所以又把它删节为现在的选译本①。这以前，我曾看见有人把这诗集选译过，但似乎错得太多，因此我译时不曾拿它来参考。

近来小诗十分发达。它们的作者大半都是直接或间接受泰戈尔此集的影响的。此集的介绍，对于没有机会得读原文的，至少总有些贡献。

这诗集的一部分译稿是积了许多时候的，但大部分却都是在西湖俞楼译的。

我在此谢谢叶圣陶、徐玉诺二君。他们替我很仔细地校读过这部译文，并且供给了许多重要的意见给我。

郑振铎

一九二三、六、二六

---

① 此次出版的《飞鸟集》，是增补完备的全译本。——编者注。

目录

第1章· 夏天的飞鸟

001·

夏天的飞鸟，
飞到我的窗前唱歌，
又飞去了。

秋天的黄叶，
它们没有什么可唱，
只叹息一声，
飞落在那里。

Stray birds of summer
come to my window to sing
and fly away.

And yellow leaves of autumn,
which have no songs,
flutter and fall there
with a sigh.

世界上的
一队小小的
漂泊者呀，

请留下
你们的足印
在我的文字里。

O Troupe
of little vagrants
of the world,

leave
your footprints
in my words.

003 ·

世界
对着它的爱人，
把它浩瀚的面具揭下了。

它变小了，
小如一首歌，
小如一回永恒的接吻。

The world

puts off its mask of vastness

to its lover.

It becomes small

as one song,

as one kiss of the eternal.

是
大地的泪点，
使她的微笑保持着
青春不谢。

It is

the tears of the earth

that keep her smiles

in bloom.

广漠无垠的沙漠
热烈地追求着一叶绿草的爱，
但她摇摇头，
笑着飞开了。

The mighty desert

is burning for the love of a blade of grass

who shakes her head

and laughs and flies away.

如果你
因失去了太阳
而流泪，
那么你也将失去群星了。

If you
shed tears
when you miss the sun,
you also miss the stars.

跳舞着的流水呀，
在你旅途中的泥沙，
要求你的歌声，
你的流动呢。
你肯挟跛足的泥沙而俱下么？

The sands in your way

beg for your song

and your movement,

dancing water.

Will you carry the burden of their lameness?

她热切的脸，
如夜雨似的，
搅扰着我的梦魂。

Her wishful face

haunts my dreams

like the rain at night.

600

有一次，
我们梦见大家都是不相识的。
我们醒了，
却知道我们原来是相亲相爱的。

Once

we dreamt that we were strangers.

We wake up

to find that we were dear to each other.

忧思在我的心里平静下去，
正如暮色降临在寂静的山林中。

Sorrow is hushed into peace in my heart

like the evening among the silent trees.

011 .

有些看不见的手，
如懒懒的微飔的，
正在我的心上奏着
潺湲的乐声。

Some unseen fingers,

like an idle breeze,

are playing upon my heart

the music of the ripples.

"海水呀，你说的是什么？"
"是永恒的疑问。"
"天空呀，你回答的话是什么？"
"是永恒的沉默。"

What language is thine, O sea?

The language of eternal question.

What language is thy answer, O sky?

The language of eternal silence.

静静地听，
我的心呀，
听那世界的低语，
这是它对你求爱的表示呀。

Listen,

my heart,

to the whispers of the world with which

it makes love to you.

创造的神秘，
有如夜间的黑暗
——是伟大的。
而知识的幻影，
不过如晨间之雾。

The mystery of creation
is like the darkness of night
—it is great.
Delusions of knowledge
are like the fog of the morning.

不要
因为峭壁是高的，
而让你的爱情坐在峭壁上。

Do not

seat your love upon a precipice

because it is high.

我今晨坐在窗前，
世界如一个路人的似的，
停留了一会儿，
向我点点头又走过去了。

I sit at my window this morning

where the world like a passer-by

stops for a moment,

nods to me and goes.

这些微飔，

是绿叶的簌簌之声呀；

它们在我的心里愉悦地微语着。

There little thoughts

are the rustle of leaves;

they have their whisper of joy in my mind.

你看不见你的真相，
你所看见的
只是你的影子。

What you are you do not see,
what you see
is your shadow.

神呀，

我的那些愿望真是愚傻呀，

它们杂在你的歌声中喧叫着呢。

让我只是静听着吧。

My wishes are fools,

they shout across thy song,

my Master.

Let me but listen.

我不能
选择那最好的。
是那最好的
选择我。

I cannot

choose the best.

The best

chooses me.

那些把灯
背在背上的人，
把他们的影子投到了
自己前面。

They throw their shadows

before them

who carry their lantern

on their back.

我的存在，
对我是一个永久的神奇，
这就是生活。

That I exist

is a perpetual surprise

which is life.

"我们，
萧萧的树叶，
都有声响回答那暴风雨。
你是谁呢，
那样地沉默着？"
"我不过是一朵花。"

"We,
the rustling leaves,
have a voice that answers the storms,
but who are you
so silent?"
"I am a mere flower."

休息与工作的关系，
正如
眼睑与眼睛的关系。

Rest belongs to the work

as

the eyelids to the eyes.

025.

人是一个初生的孩子，
他的力量，
就是生长的力量。

Man is a born child,

his power

is the power of growth.

上帝希望我们酬答他，
在于他送给我们的花朵，
而不在于太阳和土地。

God expects answers
for the flowers he sends us,
not for the sun the earth.

光明如同一个裸体的孩子，

快快活活地在绿叶当中游戏，

它不知道人是会欺诈的。

The light that plays,

like a naked child,

among the green leaves happily

knows not that man can lie.

啊，美呀，

在爱中找你自己吧，

不要到你镜子的谄谀去找寻。

O Beauty,

find thyself in love,

not in the flattery of thy mirror.

我的心把她的波浪在世界的海岸上冲激着，
以热泪在上面写着她的题记：
"我爱你。"

My heart beats her waves at the shore of the world
and writes upon it her signature in tears with the words,
"I love thee."

"月儿呀，
你在等候什么呢？"
"向
我将让位给他的
太阳致敬。"

Moon,

for what do you wait?

To

salute the sun for

whom I must make way.

绿树长到了我的窗前，
仿佛是喑哑的大地发出的
渴望的声音。

The trees come up to my window
like the yearning voice
of the dumb earth.

神
自己的清晨，
在他自己看来也是新奇的。

His own mornings

are new surprises

to God.

生命
从世界得到资产，
爱情
使它得到价值。

Life finds its wealth
by the claims of the world,
and its worth
by the claims of love.

枯竭的河床，
并不感谢
它的过去。

The dry river-bed
finds no thanks
for its past.

035.

鸟儿
愿为一朵云。
云儿
愿为一只鸟。

The bird

wishes it were a cloud.

The cloud

wishes it were a bird.

瀑布歌唱道：
"我得到自由时，
便有了歌声了。"

The waterfall sing,
"I find my song,
when I find my freedom."

037.

我说不出
这心为什么那样默默地颓丧着。
是为了它那不曾要求、
不曾知道、
不曾记得的小小的需求。

I cannot tell

why this heart languishes in silence.

It is for small needs it never asks,

or knows

or remembers.

妇人，

你在料理家务的时候，

你的手足歌唱着，

正如山间的溪水歌唱着在小石中流过。

Woman,

when you move about in your household service

your limbs sing

like a hill stream among its pebbles.

当太阳横过西方的海面时，
对着东方
留下他的最后的敬礼。

The sun goes to cross the Western sea,

leaving its last salutation

to the East.

不要因为你自己
没有胃口
而去责备你的食物。

Do not blame your food

because you have

no appetite.

041.

群树
如表示大地的愿望似的，
踮起脚来向天空窥望。

The trees,

like the longings of the earth,

stand a tiptoe to peep at the heaven.

你微微地笑着，
不同我说什么话。
而我觉得，
为了这个，
我已等待得久了。

You smiled
and talked to me of nothing
and I felt that
for this
I had been waiting long.

水里的游鱼是沉默的，
陆地上的兽类是喧闹的，
空中的飞鸟是歌唱着的。

但是，
人类却兼有海里的沉默，
地上的喧闹与空中的音乐。

The fish in the water is silent,

the animal on the earth is noisy,

the bird in the air is singing.

But

Man has in him the silence of the sea,

the noise of the earth and the music of the air.

世界
在踌躇之心的琴弦上
跑过去，
奏出忧郁的乐声。

The world

rushes on

over the strings of the lingering heart

making the music of sadness.

他把他的刀剑当作他的上帝。
当他的刀剑胜利时
他自己却失败了。

He has made his weapons his gods.

When his weapons win

he is defeated himself.

神
从创造中
找到他自己。

God
finds himself
by creating.

阴影
戴上她的面幕，
秘密地，温顺地，
用她的沉默的爱的脚步，
跟在"光"后边。

Shadow,

with her veil drawn,

follows Light

in secret meekness,

with her silent steps of love.

群星
不怕
显得像萤火那样。

The stars
are not afraid
to appear like fireflies.

049.

谢谢神，
我不是一个权力的轮子，
而是被压在这轮子下的
活人之一。

I thank thee

that I am none of the wheels of power

but I am one with the living creatures

that are crushed by it.

心是尖锐的，
不是宽博的，
它执着在每一点上，
却并不活动。

The mind,

sharp but not broad,

sticks at every point

but does not move.

你的偶像委散在尘土中了，
这可证明
神的尘土比你的偶像还伟大。

You idol is shattered in the dust
to prove that
God's dust is greater than your idol.

人不能
在他的历史中表现出他自己，
他在历史中奋斗着露出头角。

Man does not
reveal himself in his history,
he struggles up through it.

玻璃灯因为瓦灯叫做它表兄而责备瓦灯。
但明月出来时，
玻璃灯却温和地微笑着，
叫明月为
——"我亲爱的，亲爱的姐姐。"

While the glass lamp rebukes the earthen for

calling it cousin,

the moon rises,

and the glass lamp,

with a bland smile,

calls her,

—"My dear, dear sister."

我们如海鸥之与波涛相遇似的，
遇见了，
走近了。

海鸥飞去，
波涛滚滚地流开，
我们也分别了。

Like the meeting of the seagulls and the waves

we meet

and come near.

The seagulls fly off,

the waves roll away

and we depart.

我的白昼已经完了，
我像一只泊在海滩上的小船，
谛听着晚潮跳舞的乐声。

My day is done,

and I am like a boat drawn on the beach,

listening to the dance-music of the tide in the evening.

我们的生命是天赋的，
我们唯有献出生命，
才能得到生命。

Life is given to us,

we earn it

by giving it.

当我们是大为谦卑的时候，
便是我们最接近伟大的时候。

We come nearest to the great
when we are great in humility.

麻雀
看见孔雀负担着它的翎尾，
替它担忧。

The sparrow

is sorry for

the peacock at the burden of its tail.

决不要

害怕刹那

——永恒之声这样唱着。

Never

be afraid of the moments

—thus sings the voice of the everlasting.

飓风于无路之中寻求最短之路，
又突然地在"无何有之国"
终止了它的追求。

The hurricane seeks the shortest road by the no-road,

and suddenly ends its search

in the Nowhere.

061 ·

在我自己的杯中，
饮了我的酒吧，
朋友。

一倒在别人的杯里，
这酒的腾跳的泡沫便要消失了。

Take my wine

in my own cup,

friend.

It loses its wreath of foam

when poured into that of others.

"完全"
为了对"不全"的爱，
把自己装饰得美丽。

The Perfect

decks itself in beauty

for the love of the Imperfect.

063.

神对人说道：
"我医治你所以伤害你，
爱你所以惩罚你。"

God says to man,

"I heal you therefore I hurt,

love you therefore punish."

谢谢火焰给你光明，
但是不要忘了那执灯的人，
他是坚忍地站在黑暗当中呢。

Thank the flame for its light,

but do not forget the lampholder

standing in the shade with constancy of patience.

小草呀，
你的足步虽小，
但是你拥有你足下的土地。

Tiny grass,

your steps are small,

but you possess the earth under your tread.

990.

幼花的蓓蕾开放了，
它叫道：
"亲爱的世界呀，
请不要萎谢了。"

The infant flower opens its bud
and cries,
"Dear World,
please do not fade."

神
对于那些大帝国会感到厌恶，
却决不会厌恶那些小小的花朵。

God
grows weary of great kingdoms,
but never of little flowers.

错误
经不起失败，
但是真理却不怕失败。

Wrong

cannot afford defeat

but Right can.

690

瀑布唱道：
"虽然渴者只要少许的水便够了，
我却很快活地给予了我的全部的水。"

"I give my whole water in joy,"

sings the waterfall,

"though little of it is enough for the thirsty."

把那些花朵抛掷上去的
那一阵子无休无止的狂欢大喜的劲儿，
其源泉是在哪里呢？

Where is the fountain
that throws up these flowers
in a ceaseless outbreak of ecstasy?

第 2 章 · 生如夏花

071 ·

樵夫的斧头，
问树要斧柄。
树便给了他。

The woodcutter's axe
begged for its handle from the tree.
The tree gave it.

这寂独的黄昏，
幕着雾与雨，
我在我的心的孤寂里，
感觉到它的叹息。

In my solitude of heart
I feel the sigh
of this widowed evening
veiled with mist and rain.

贞操
是从丰富的爱情中生出来的
财富。

Chastity

is a wealth

that comes from abundance of love.

雾，
像爱情一样，
在山峰的心上游戏，
生出种种美丽的变幻。

The mist,

like love,

plays upon the heart of the hills

and bring out surprises of beauty.

我们
把世界看错了，
反说他欺骗我们。

We
read the world wrong
and say that it deceives us.

诗人的飙风，

正出经海洋森林，

追求它自己的歌声。

The poet wind

is out over the sea

and the forest to seek his own voice.

每一个孩子出生时
都带来信息说：
神对人并未灰心失望。

Every child comes
with the message
that God is not yet discouraged of man.

绿草
求她地上
的伴侣。

树木
求他天空
的寂寞。

The grass
seeks her crowd
in the earth.

The tree
seeks his solitude
of the sky.

人
对他自己
建筑起堤防来。

Man
barricades
against himself.

我的朋友，
你的语声
飘荡在我的心里，
像那海水的低吟声，
缭绕在静听着的松林之间。

Your voice,

my friend,

wanders in my heart,

like the muffled sound of the sea

among these listening pines.

081.

这个不可见的黑暗之火焰，
以繁星为其火花的，
到底是什么呢？

What is
this unseen flame of darkness
whose sparks are the stars?

使生
如夏花之绚烂，
死如
秋叶之静美。

Let life be beautiful,

like summer flowers

and death

like autumn leaves.

083.

那想做好人的，
在门外敲着门；
那爱人的，
看见门敞开着。

He who wants to do good
knocks at the gate;
he who loves
finds the gate open.

在死的时候，
众多合而为一；
在生的时候，
一化为众多。

神死了的时候，
宗教便将合而为一。

In death
the many becomes one;
in life
the one becomes many.

Religion will be one
when God is dead.

085.

艺术家是自然的情人，
所以他是自然的奴隶，
也是自然的主人。

The artist is the lover of Nature,

therefore he is her slave

and her master.

"你离我有多远呢，
果实呀？"
"我藏在你心里呢，
花呀。"

"How far are you from me,
O Fruit?"
"I am hidden in your heart,
O Flower."

087.

这个渴望是为了
那个在黑夜里感觉得到，
在大白天里却看不见的人。

This longing is for

the one who is felt in the dark,

but not seen in the day.

露珠对湖水说道：
"你是在荷叶下面的大露珠，
我是在荷叶上面的较小的露珠。"

"You are the big drop of dew under the lotus leaf,
I am the smaller one on its upper side,"
said the dewdrop to the lake.

089.

刀鞘
保护刀的锋利，
它自己则满足于它的迟钝。

The scabbard

is content to be dull

when it protects the keenness of the sword.

在黑暗中，

"一"视若一体；

在光亮中，

"一"便视若众多。

In darkness

the One appears as uniform;

in the light

the One appears as manifold.

091·

大地
借助于绿草，
显出她自己的殷勤好客。

The great earth
makes herself hospitable
with the help of the grass.

绿叶的生与死
乃是旋风的急骤的旋转，
它的更广大的旋转的圈子，
乃是在天上繁星之间徐缓的转动。

The birth and death of the leaves
are the rapid whirls of the eddy
whose wider circles
move slowly among stars.

093．

权势对世界说道：

"你是我的。"

世界便把权势囚禁在她的宝座下面。

爱情对世界说道：

"我是你的。"

世界便给予爱情以在她屋内来往的自由。

Power said to the world,

"You are mine."

The world kept it prisoner on her throne.

Love said to the world,

"I am thine."

The world gave it the freedom of her house.

浓雾仿佛是大地的愿望。
它藏起了太阳，
而太阳原是她所呼求的。

The mist is like the earth's desire.

It hides the sun

for whom she cries.

095.

安静些吧，
我的心，
这些大树都是祈祷者呀。

Be still,

my heart,

these great trees are prayers.

瞬刻的喧声，
讥笑着
永恒的音乐。

The noise of the Moment

scoffs at

the music of the Eternal.

097.

我想起了
浮泛在生与爱与死的川流上的
许多别的时代，
以及这些时代之被遗忘，
我便感觉到离开尘世的自由了。

I think of

other ages

that floated upon the stream of life and love and death

and are forgotten,

and I feel the freedom of passing away.

我灵魂里的忧郁
就是她的新婚的面纱。
这面纱等候着
在夜间卸去。

The sadness of my soul
is her bride's veil.
It waits
to be lifted in the night.

660

死之印记给生的钱币以价值；
使它能够
用生命来购买那真正的宝物。

Death's stamp gives value to the coin of life;

making it possible

to buy with life what is truly precious.

白云

谦逊地站在天之一隅。

晨光

给它戴上霞彩。

The cloud

stood humbly in a corner of the sky.

The morning

crowned it with splendour.

101·

尘土受到损辱，
却以她的花朵
来报答。

The dust receives insult

and in return

offers her flowers.

只管走过去，
不必逗留着采了花朵来保存，
因为一路上花朵自会继续开放的。

Do not linger to gather flowers to keep them,

but walk on,

for flowers will keep themselves blooming all your way.

根
是地下的枝。
枝
是空中的根。

Roots

are the branches down in the earth.

Branches

are roots in the air.

远远去了的夏之音乐，

翱翔于秋间，

寻找它的旧垒。

The music of the far-away summer

flutters around the Autumn

seeking its former nest.

不要从你自己的袋里掏出勋绩
借给你的朋友，
这是污辱他的。

Do not insult your friend
by lending him merits from
your own pocket.

无名的日子的感触，
攀缘在我的心上，
正像那绿色的苔藓，
攀缘在老树的周身。

The touch of the nameless days

clings to my heart

like mosses

round the old tree.

107.

回声嘲笑着她的原声，
以证明
她是原声。

The echo mocks her origin
to prove
she is the original.

当富贵利达的人
夸说他得到神的特别恩惠时，
上帝却羞了。

God is ashamed

when the prosperous

boasts of His special favour.

我投射我自己的影子在我的路上，
因为我有一盏
还没有燃点起来的明灯。

I cast my own shadow upon my path,

because I have a lamp

that has not been lighted.

人
走进喧哗的群众里去，
为的是
要淹没他自己的沉默的呼号。

Man

goes into the noisy crowed

to

drown his own clamour of silence.

终止于衰竭是
"死亡"，
但"圆满"却终止于
无穷。

That which ends in exhaustion

is death,

but the perfect ending

is in the endless.

太阳
只穿一件朴素的光衣，
白云
却披了灿烂的裙裾。

The sun

has his simple robe of light.

The clouds

are decked with gorgeousness.

山峰如群儿之喧嚷，
举起他们的双臂，
想去捉天上的星星。

The hills are like shouts of children

who raise their arms,

trying to catch stars.

道路虽然拥挤，
却是寂寞的，
因为它是不被爱的。

The road is lonely

in its crowd

for it is not loved.

权威以它的恶行自夸，
落下的黄叶与浮游的云片
却在笑它。

The power that boasts of its mischiefs is laughed at

by the yellow leaves that fall,

and clouds that pass by.

今天大地在太阳光里向我营营哼鸣，
像一个织着布的妇人，
用一种已经被忘却的语言，
哼着一些古代的歌曲。

The earth hums to me today in the sun,

like a woman at her spinning,

some ballad of the ancient time

in a forgotten tongue.

绿草
是无愧于
它所生长的伟大世界的。

The grass-blade
is worthy of the great world
where it grows.

梦
是一个一定要谈话的妻子。
睡眠
是一个沉默忍受的丈夫。

Dream

is a wife who must talk.

Sleep

is a husband who silently suffers.

119·

夜与逝去的日子接吻，
轻轻地在他耳旁说道：
"我是死，
是你的母亲。
我就要给你以新的生命。"

The night kisses the fading day

whispering to his ear,

I am death,

your mother.

I am to give you fresh birth.

黑夜呀，

我感觉到你的美了。

你的美如一个可爱的妇人，

当她把灯灭了的时候。

I feel thy beauty,

dark night,

like that of the loved woman

when she has put out the lamp.

121.

我把在那些
已逝去的世界上的繁荣
带到我的世界上来。

I carry in my world
that flourishes the worlds
that have failed.

亲爱的朋友呀，

当我静听着海涛时，

我好几次在暮色深沉的黄昏里，

在这个海岸上，

感到你的伟大思想的沉默了。

Dear friend,

I feel the silence of your great thoughts

of many a deepening eventide

on this beach

when I listen to these waves.

鸟以为
把鱼举在空中
是一种慈善的举动。

The bird thinks

it is an act of kindness

to give the fish a life in the air.

夜对太阳说道：
"在月亮中，
你送了你的情书给我。"
"我已在绿草上留下了我的流着泪点的回答了。"

"In the moon

thou sendest thy love letters to me,"

said the night to the sun.

"I leave my answers in tears upon the grass."

125.

伟人是一个天生的孩子，

当他死时，

他把他的伟大的孩提时代给了世界。

The great is a born child;

when he dies

he gives his great childhood to the world.

不是槌的打击，
乃是水的载歌载舞，
使鹅卵石臻于完美。

Not hammer-strokes,

but dance of the water

sings the pebbles into perfection.

蜜蜂从花中啜蜜，
离开时
营营地道谢。
浮华的蝴蝶却相信
花是应该向他道谢的。

Bees sip honey from flowers

and hum their thanks

when they leave.

The gaudy butterfly is sure

that the flowers owe thanks to him.

如果你不等待着要说出
完全的真理，
那末把真话说出来是很容易的。

To be outspoken is easy

when you do not wait to speak

the complete truth.

"可能"问"不可能"道：

"你住在什么地方呢？"

"不可能"回答道：

"在那无能为力者的梦境里。"

Asks the Possible to the Impossible,

Where is your dwelling-place?

In the dreams of the impotent,

comes the answer.

如果你
把所有的错误都关在外时，
真理也要被关在外面了。

If you

shut your door to all errors

truth will be shut out.

131.

我听见有些东西
在我心的忧闷后面萧萧作响，
——我不能看见它们。

I hear some rustle of things
behind my sadness of heart,
—I cannot see them.

闲暇在动作时
便是工作。
静止的海水荡动时
便成波涛。

Leisure in its activity

is work.

The stillness of the sea

stirs in waves.

133.

绿叶
恋爱时
便成了花。

花
崇拜时
便成了果实。

The leaf

becomes flower

when it loves.

The flower

becomes fruit

when it worships.

埋在地下的
树根
使树枝产生果实，
却不要求什么报酬。

The roots

below the earth

claim no rewards

for making the branches fruitful.

135.

阴雨的黄昏，
风无休止地吹着。
我看着摇曳的树枝，
想念万物的伟大。

This rainy evening the wind
is restless.
I look at the swaying branches
and ponder over the greatness of all things.

子夜的风雨，
如一个巨大的孩子，
在不合时宜的黑夜里醒来，
开始游戏和喧闹。

Storm of midnight,

like a giant child

awakened in the untimely dark,

has begun to play and shout.

137.

海呀，
你这暴风雨的孤寂的新妇呀，
你虽掀起波浪追随你的情人，
但是无用呀。

Thou raisest thy waves

vainly to follow thy lover,

O sea,

thou lonely bride of the storm.

文字对工作说道：
"我惭愧我的空虚。"
工作对文字说道：
"当我看见你的时候，
我便知道我是怎样地贫乏了。"

I am ashamed of my emptiness,

said the Word to the Work.

I know how poor I am

when I see you,

said the Work to the Word.

时间是变化的财富。
时钟模仿它，
却只有变化而无财富。

Time is the wealth of change,

but the clock in its parody

makes it mere change and no wealth.

真理穿了衣裳，
觉得事实太拘束了。
在想象中，
她却转动得很舒畅。

Truth in her dress

finds facts too tight.

In fiction

she moves with ease.

当我到这里那里旅行着时，

路呀，

我厌倦你了；

但是现在，

当你引导我到各处去时，

我便爱上你，

与你结婚了。

When I travelled to here and to there,

I was tired of thee,

O Road,

but now

when thou leadest me to everywhere

I am wedded to thee

in love.

让我设想，

在群星之中，

有一颗星是指导着我的生命通过不可知的黑暗的。

Let me think

that there is one among those stars

that guides my life through the dark unknown.

143.

妇人，
你用了你美丽的手指，
触着我的什物，
秩序便如音乐似地生出来了。

Woman,
with the grace of your fingers
you touched my things
and order came out like music.

一个忧郁的声音，
筑巢于逝水似的年华中。
它在夜里向我唱道：
"我爱你。"

One sad voice

has its nest among the ruins of the years.

It sings to me in the night,

I loved you.

145·

燃着的火，
以它熊熊的光焰警告我不要走近它。
把我从潜藏在灰中的余烬里
救出来吧。

The flaming fire

warns me off by its own glow.

Save me from

the dying embers hidden under ashes.

我有群星在天上。
但是，
唉，
我屋里的小灯却没有点亮。

I have my stars in the sky.

But

oh

for my little lamp unlit in my house.

147.

死文字的尘土
沾着你。
用沉默
去洗净你的灵魂吧。

The dust of the dead words

clings to thee.

Wash thy soul

with silence.

生命里留了
许多罅隙，
从中送来了
死之忧郁的音乐。

Gaps

are left in life through

which comes the sad music of death.

世界已在早晨敞开了它的光明之心。
出来吧，
我的心，
带着你的爱去与它相会。

The world has opened its heart of light in the morning.

Come out,

my heart,

with thy love to meet it.

我的思想随着这些闪耀的绿叶而闪耀；
我的心灵因为这些日光的抚慰而歌唱；
我的生命因为偕了万物一同浮泛在空间的蔚蓝、
时间的墨黑而感到欢快。

My thoughts shimmer with these shimmering leaves

and my heart sings with the touch of this sunlight;

my life is glad to be floating with all things into the blue of space,

into the dark of time.

神的巨大的权威
是在柔和的微雨里，
而不在狂风暴雨之中。

God's great power

is in the gentle breeze,

not in the storm.

在梦中，
一切事都散漫着，
都压着我，
但这不过是一个梦呀。

但我醒来时，
我便将觉得这些事都已聚集在你那里，
我也便将自由了。

This is a dream
in which
things are all loose
and they oppress.

I shall find them gathered in thee
when I awake
and shall be free.

153.

落日问道：
"有谁在继续我的职务呢？"
瓦灯说道：
"我要尽我所能地做去，
我的主人。"

Who is there to take up my duties?

asked the setting sun.

I shall do what I can,

my Master,

said the earthen lamp.

采着花瓣时，
得不到
花的美丽。

By plucking her petals
you do not gather
the beauty of the flower.

155.

沉默蕴蓄着语声，
正如
鸟巢拥围着睡鸟。

Silence will carry your voice

like

the nest that holds the sleeping birds.

大的
不怕与小的
同游。
居中的却远而避之。

The Great walks

with the Small

without fear.

The Middling keeps aloof.

157.

夜
秘密地把花开放了，
却让白日
去领受谢词。

The night

opens the flowers in secret

and allows the day

to get thanks.

权力
认为牺牲者的痛苦
是忘恩负义。

Power

takes as ingratitude

the writhings of its victims.

159.

当我们以我们的充实为乐时，

那末，

我们便能很快乐地跟我们的果实分手了。

When we rejoice in our fullness,

then

we can part with our fruits with joy.

雨点吻着大地，

微语道：

"我们是你的思家的孩子，

母亲，

现在从天上回到你这里来了。"

The raindrops kissed the earth and whispered,

"—We are thy homesick children,

mother,

come back to thee from the heaven."

蛛网
好像要捉露点，
却捉住了苍蝇。

The cobweb
pretends to catch dewdrops
and catches flies.

爱情呀，

当你手里拿着点亮了的痛苦之灯走来时，

我能够看见你的脸，

而且以你为幸福。

Love!

When you come with the burning lamp of pain in your hand,

I can see your face

and know you as bliss.

萤火对天上的星道：
"学者说你的光明，
总有一天会消灭的。"
天上的星不回答它。

The learned say

that your lights will one day be no more,

said the firefly to the stars.

The stars made no answer.

在黄昏的微光里，
有那清晨的鸟儿
来到了我的沉默的鸟巢里。

In the dusk of the evening
the bird of some early dawn
comes to the nest of my silence.

165.

思想掠过我的心上，
如一群野鸭飞过天空。
我听见它们鼓翼之声了。

Thoughts pass in my mind

like flocks of lucks in the sky.

I hear the voice of their wings.

沟洫总喜欢想：
河流的存在，
是专为它供给水流的。

The canal loves to think

that rivers exist

solely to supply it with water.

世界
以它的痛苦同我接吻，
而要求歌声作报酬。

The world

has kissed my soul with its pain,

asking for its return in songs.

压迫着我的，
到底是我的想要外出的灵魂呢，
还是那世界的灵魂，
敲着我心的门，
想要进来呢？

That which oppresses me,

is it my soul trying to come out in the open,

or the soul of the world

knocking at my heart

for its entrance?

169 ·

思想
以它自己的语言
喂养它自己
而成长起来。

Thought

feeds itself

with its own words

and grows.

我把我的心之碗
轻轻浸入这沉默的时刻中，
它盛满了爱了。

I have dipped the vessel of my heart

into this silent hour;

it has filled with love.

171·

或者你在工作，
或者你没有。
当你不得不说：
"让我们做些事吧"时，
那末就要开始胡闹了。

Either you have work

or you have not.

When you have to say,

"Let us do something",

then begins mischief.

向日葵
羞于把无名的花朵
看作它的同胞。
太阳升上来了，
向它微笑，
道："你好么，我的宝贝儿？"

The sunflower
blushed to own the nameless flower
as her kin.
The sun rose
and smiled on it,
saying,"Are you well, my darling?"

173.

"谁如命运似地
催着我向前走呢？"
"那是我自己，
在身背后大跨步走着。"

"Who drives me forward

like fate?"

"The Myself

striding on my back."

云
把水倒在河的水杯里，
它们自己却藏在
远山之中。

The clouds

fill the watercups of the river,

hiding themselves

in the distant hills.

175·

我一路走去，
从我的水瓶中漏出水来。
只留下极少极少的水供我回家使用了。

I spill water from my water jar

as I walk on my way,

Very little remains for my home.

杯中的水是光辉的；
海中的水却是黑色的。
小理可以用文字来说清楚，
大理却只有沉默。

The water in a vessel is sparkling;

the water in the sea is dark.

The small truth has words that are clear;

the great truth has great silence.

你的微笑是你自己田园里的花，
你的谈吐是你自己山上的松林的萧萧；
但是你的心呀，
却是那个女人，
那个我们全都认识的女人。

Your smile was the flowers of your own fields,

your talk was the rustle of your own mountain pines,

but your heart

was the woman

that we all know.

我把小小的礼物
留给我所爱的人
——大的礼物却留给一切的人。

It is the little things that
I leave behind for my loved ones
—great things are for everyone.

妇人呀，
你用泪海包绕着世界的心，
正如大海包绕着大地。

Woman,

thou hast encircled the world's heart with the depth of thy tears

as the sea has the earth.

太阳以微笑向我问候。

雨，

它的忧郁的妹妹，

向我的心谈话。

The sunshine greets me with a smile.

The rain,

his sad sister,

talks to my heart.

我的昼间之花，
落下它那被遗忘的花瓣。
在黄昏中，
这花成熟为一颗记忆的金果。

My flower of the day

dropped its petals forgotten.

In the evening

it ripens into a golden fruit of memory.

我像那夜间之路，
正静悄悄地
谛听着记忆的足音。

I am like the road in the night

listening to the footfalls of its memories

in silence.

183.

黄昏的天空，
在我看来，
像一扇窗户，
一盏灯火，
灯火背后的一次等待。

The evening sky

to me

is like a window,

and a lighted lamp,

and a waiting behind it.

184.

太急于做好事
的人，
反而找不到时间去做好事。

He who is

too busy doing good

finds no time to be good.

飞 鸟 集
- 189 -

185.

我是秋云，
空空地不载着雨水，
但在成熟的稻田中，
看见了我的充实。

I am the autumn cloud,

empty of rain,

see my fullness

in the field of ripened rice.

他们嫉妒，

他们残杀，

人反而称赞他们。

然而上帝却害了羞，

匆匆地把他的记忆埋藏在绿草下面。

They hated

and killed

and men praised them.

But God in shame

hastens to hide its memory under the green grass.

脚趾乃是
舍弃了其过去
的手指。

Toes are
the fingers
that have forsaken their past.

黑暗向光明旅行，
但是
盲者却向死亡旅行。

Darkness travels towards light,

but

blindness towards death.

189.

小狗
疑心大宇宙
阴谋篡夺它的位置。

.

The pet dog
suspects the universe
for scheming to take its place.

静静地坐着吧，

我的心，

不要扬起你的尘土。

让世界自己寻路向你走来。

Sit still,

my heart,

do not raise your dust.

Let the world find its way to you.

191.

弓在箭要射出之前，
低声对箭说道：
"你的自由就是我的自由。"

The bow whispers to the arrow
before it speeds forth
"Your freedom is mine."

妇人，
在你的笑声里
有着生命之泉的音乐。

Woman,

in your laughter

you have the music of the fountain of life.

全是理智的心，
恰如一柄全是锋刃的刀。
叫使用它的人手上流血。

A mind all logic

is like a knife all blade.

It makes the hand bleed that uses it.

神
爱人间的灯光
甚于他自己的大星。

God

loves man's lamp lights

better than his own great stars.

195.

这世界
乃是为美之音乐所驯服了的狂风骤雨
的世界。

This world

is the world of

wild storms kept tame with the music of beauty.

晚霞向太阳说道：
"我的心经了你的接吻，
便似金的宝箱了。"

"My heart is like the golden casket
of thy kiss,"
said the sunset cloud to the sun.

197.

接触着，
你许会杀害；
远离着，
你许会占有。

By touching
you may kill,
by keeping away
you may possess.

今天我的心是在想家了，
在想着那跨过时间之海的
那一个甜蜜的时候。

My heart is homesick today

for the one sweet hour

across the sea of time.

花朵向星辰落尽了的曙天叫道：
"我的露点全失落了。"

"I have lost my dewdrop,"

cries the flower to the morning sky that has lost all its stars.

燃烧着的木块，
熊熊地生出火光，
叫道："这是我的花朵，
我的死亡。"

The burning log

bursts in flame and cries,

—"This is my flower,

my death."

201·

黄蜂认为

邻蜂储蜜之巢太小。

它的邻人

要它去建筑一个更小的。

The wasp thinks

that the honeyhive of the neighbouring bees is too small.

His neighbours

ask him to build one still smaller.

河岸向河流说道：
"我不能留住你的波浪。"
"让我保存你的足印在我的心里吧。"

"I cannot keep your waves,"

says the bank to the river.

"Let me keep your footprints in my heart."

白日
以这小小的地球的喧扰，
淹没了整个宇宙的沉默。

The day,

with the noise of this little earth,

drowns the silence of all worlds.

歌声在天空中感到无限，

图画在地上感到无限，

诗呢，

无论在空中，在地上都是如此。

因为诗的词句含有能走动的意义与能飞翔的音乐。

The song feels the infinite in the air,

the picture in the earth,

the poem

in the air and the earth;

For its words have meaning that walks and music that soars.

205.

太阳在西方落下时，
它的早晨的东方
已静悄悄地站在它面前。

When the sun goes down to the West,

the East of his morning

stands before him in silence.

让我不要
错误地把自己放在我的世界里
而使它反对我。

Let me not

put myself wrongly to my world

and set it against me.

荣誉使我感到惭愧，
因为
我暗地里求着它。

Praise shames me,
for
I secretly beg for it.

当我没有什么事做时，
便让我不做什么事，
不受骚扰地沉入安静深处吧，
一如海水沉默时海边的暮色。

Let my doing nothing

when I have nothing to do

become untroubled in its depth of peace

like the evening in the seashore when the water is silent.

209·

少女呀，
你的纯朴，
如湖水之碧，
表现出你的真理之深邃。

Maiden,

your simplicity,

like the blueness of the lake,

reveals your depth of truth.

最好的东西
不是独来的。
它伴了所有的东西
同来。

The best

does not come alone.

It comes

with the company of the all.

第 4 章 · 鸟的歌声

211·

上帝的右手是慈爱的，
但是
他的左手却可怕。

God's right hand is gentle,

but

terrible is his left hand.

我的晚色
从陌生的树林中走来，
它用我的晓星所不懂得的
语言说话。

My evening

came among the alien trees

and spoke in a language

which my morning stars did not know.

夜之黑暗是一只口袋，
迸出
黎明的金光。

Night's darkness is a bag
that bursts with
the gold of the dawn.

我们的欲望
把彩虹的颜色
借给那只不过是云雾的人生。

Our desire

lends the colours of the rainbow

to the mere mists and vapours of life.

215.

上帝等待着，
要从人的手上把他自己的花朵
作为礼物赢得回去。

God waits

to win back his own flowers

as gifts from man's hands.

我的忧思
缠扰着我，
问我它们自己的名字。

My sad thoughts

tease me

asking me their own names.

果实的事业是尊贵的，

花的事业是甜美的；

但是让我做叶的事业吧，

叶是谦逊地专心地垂着绿荫的。

The service of the fruit is precious,

the service of the flower is sweet,

but let my service be the service of the leaves

in its shade of humble devotion.

218 ·

我的心向着阑珊的风张了帆，
要到无论何处的
荫凉之岛去。

My heart has spread its sails
to the idle winds for the shadowy island
of Anywhere.

飞 鸟 集
- 225 -

独夫们
是凶暴的，
但人民
是善良的。

Men
are cruel,
but Man
is kind.

把我当作你的杯吧，
让我为了你，
而且为了你的人而盛满水吧。

Make me thy cup
and let my fullness be for thee
and for thine.

狂风暴雨
像是在痛苦中的某个天神的哭声，
因为他的爱情被大地所拒绝。

The storm

is like the cry of some god in pain

whose love the earth refuses.

世界不会流失，

因为

死亡并不是一个罅隙。

The world does not leak

because

death is not a crack.

223.

生命因为付出了
的爱情
而更为富足。

Life has become richer

by the love

that has been lost.

我的朋友，

你伟大的心闪射出东方朝阳的光芒，

正如黎明中的一个积雪的孤峰。

My friend,

your great heart shone with the sunrise of the East

like the snowy summit of a lonely hill in the dawn.

225.

死之流泉，
使生的止水
跳跃。

The fountain of death
makes the still water
of life play.

那些有一切东西而没有您的人，
我的上帝，
在讥笑着那些没有别的东西而只有您的人呢。

Those who have everything but thee,

my God,

laugh at those who have nothing but thyself.

227.

生命的运动
在它自己的音乐里
得到它的休息。

The movement of life

has its rest

in its own music.

踢足

只能从地上扬起尘土

而不能得到收获。

Kicks

only raise dust

and not crops from the earth.

229·

我们的名字，
便是夜里海波上发出的光，
痕迹也不留就泯灭了。

Our names

are the light that glows on the sea waves at night

and then dies without leaving its signature.

让
睁眼看着玫瑰花的人
也看看它的刺。

Let him

only see the thorns

who has eyes to see the rose.

鸟翼上系了黄金，
这鸟便永不能
再在天上翱翔了。

Set the bird's wings with gold
and it will never
again soar in the sky.

我们地方的荷花又
在这陌生的水上开了花，
放出同样的清香，
只是名字换了。

The same lotus of our clime blooms here

in the alien water

with the same sweetness,

under another name.

233·

在心的远景里，
那相隔的距离显得更广阔了。

In heart's perspective

the distance looms large.

月儿把她的光明
遍照在天上，
却留着她的黑斑给她自己。

The moon has her light
all over the sky,
her dark spots to herself.

不要说：
"这是早晨了"，
别用一个"昨天"的名词把它打发掉。
你第一次看到它，
把它当作还没有名字的新生孩子吧。

Do not say,
"It is morning,"
and dismiss it with a name of yesterday.
See it for the first time
as a new-born child that has no name

青烟对天空夸口，

灰烬对大地夸口，

都以为它们是火的兄弟。

Smoke boasts to the sky,

and Ashes to the earth,

that they are brothers to the fire.

雨点向茉莉花微语道：
"把我永久地留在你的心里吧。"
茉莉花叹息了一声，
落在地上了。

The raindrop whispered to the jasmine,

"Keep me in your heart for ever."

The jasmine sighed, "Alas,"

and dropped to the ground.

238 ·

腼怩的思想呀，
不要怕我。
我是一个诗人。

Timid thoughts,
 do not be afraid of me.
I am a poet.

我的心在朦胧的沉默里，
似乎充满了蟋蟀的鸣声
——声音的灰暗的暮色。

The dim silence of my mind

seems filled with crickets' chirp

—the grey twilight of sound.

爆竹呀，

你对群星的侮蔑，

又跟了你自己回到地上来了。

Rockets,

your insult to the stars

follows yourself back to the earth.

您曾经带领着我，
穿过我的白天的拥挤不堪的旅程，
而到达了我的黄昏的孤寂之境。
在通宵的寂静里，
我等待着它的意义。

Thou hast led me

through my crowded travels of the day

to my evening's loneliness.

I wait for its meaning

through the stillness of the night.

蟋蟀的唧唧，
夜雨的淅沥，
从黑暗中传到我的耳边，
好似我已逝的少年时代沙沙地来到我
的梦境中。

The cricket's chirp

and the patter of rain

come to me through the dark,

like the rustle of dreams

from my past youth.

243.

真理之川
从它的错误之沟渠中
流过。

The stream of truth

flows through

its channels of mistakes.

我们的生命就似渡过一个大海，
我们都相聚在这个狭小的舟中。
死时，
我们便到了岸，
各往各的世界去了。

This life is the crossing of a sea,

where we meet in the same narrow ship.

In death

we reach the shore

and go to our different worlds.

鸟的歌声
是曙光从大地反响过去
的回声。

The bird-song

is the echo of

the morning light back from the earth.

晨光

问毛茛道：

"你是骄傲得不肯和我接吻么？"

"Are you too proud to kiss me?"

the morning light

asks the buttercup.

小花问道：

"我要怎样地对你唱，

怎样地崇拜你呢？

太阳呀？"

太阳答道：

"只要你用你的纯洁的素朴的沉默。"

"How may I sing to thee

and worship,

O Sun?"

asked the little flower.

"By the simple silence of thy purity,"

answered the sun.

当人
是兽时，
他比兽还坏。

Man
is worse than an animal
when he is an animal.

黑云
受光的接吻时
便变成天上的花朵。

Dark clouds

become heaven's flowers

when kissed by light.

不要让
刀锋讥笑它柄子
的拙钝。

Let not

the sword-blade mock its handle

for being blunt.

夜的沉默，
如一个深深的灯盏，
银河便是它燃着的灯光。

The night's silence,

like a deep lamp,

is burning with the light of its milky way.

死像大海的无限的歌声，

日夜

冲击着生命的光明岛的四周。

Around the sunny island of Life swells

day and night death's

limitless song of the sea.

花瓣似的山峰
在饮着日光，
这山岂不像一朵花吗？

Is not this mountain like a flower,

with its petals of hill,

drinking the sunlight?

"真实"的含义被误解，

轻重被倒置，

那就成了"不真实"。

The real with its meaning read wrong

and emphasis misplaced

is the unreal.

我的心呀，
从世界的流动
找你的美吧，
正如那小船得到风与水的优美似的。

Find your beauty,

my heart,

from the world's movement,

like the boat that has the grace of the wind and the water.

眼不能以视来骄人，
却以它们的眼镜来骄人。

The eyes are not proud of their sight
but of their eyeglasses.

我住在我的这个小小的世界里，
生怕使它再缩小一丁点儿。
把我抬举到您的世界里去吧，
让我有高高兴兴地失去我的一切的自由。

I live in this little world of mine

and am afraid to make it the least less.

Life me into thy world

and let me have the freedom gladly to lose my all.

虚伪
永远不能凭借它生长在权力中
而变成真实。

The false

can never grow into truth

by growing in power.

我的心，
同着它的歌的拍拍舐岸的波浪，
渴望着要抚爱这个阳光熙和的绿色世界。

My heart,

with its lapping waves of son,

longs to caress this green world of the sunny day.

道旁的草，

爱那天上的星吧，

那末，

你的梦境便可在花朵里实现了。

Wayside grass,

love the star,

then

your dreams will come out in flowers.

让你的音乐
如一柄利刃，
直刺入市井喧扰的心中吧。

Let your music,

like a sword,

pierce the noise of the market to its heart.

这树的颤动之叶，
触动着我的心，
像一个婴儿的手指。

The trembling leaves of this tree
touch my heart
like the fingers of an infant child.

263 ·

小花
睡在尘土里。
它寻求
蛱蝶走的道路。

The little flower

lies in the dust.

It sought

the path of the butterfly.

我是在道路纵横的世界上。

夜来了。

打开您的门吧，

家之世界啊！

I am in the world of the roads.

The night comes.

Open thy gate,

thou world of the home.

265.

我已经唱过了您的白天的歌。
在黄昏的时候，
让我拿着您的灯走过风雨飘摇的道路吧。

I have sung the songs of thy day.

In the evening

let me carry thy lamp through the stormy path.

我不要求你进我的屋里。
你且到我无量的孤寂里来吧，
我的爱人！

I do not ask thee into the house.
Come into my infinite loneliness,
my Lover.

死亡隶属于生命，
正与出生一样。
举足是在走路，
正如落足也是在走路。

Death belongs to life

as birth does.

The walk is in the raising of the foot

as in the laying of it down.

我已经学会了你在花与阳光里

微语的意义。

——再教我明白你在苦与死中所说的话吧。

I have learnt the simple meaning of

thy whispers in flowers and sunshine

—teach me to know thy words in pain and death.

269.

夜的花朵来晚了，
当早晨吻着她时，
她战栗着，
叹息了一声，
萎落在地上了。

The night's flower was late
when the morning kissed her,
she shivered
and sighed
and dropped to the ground.

从万物的愁苦中，
我听见了"永恒母亲"
的呻吟。

Through the sadness of all things
I hear the crooning
of the Eternal Mother.

271.

大地呀，
我到你岸上时是一个陌生人，
住在你屋内时是一个宾客，
离开你的门时是一个朋友。

I came to your shore as a stranger,

I lived in your house as a guest,

I leave your door as a friend,

my earth.

当我去时，
让我的思想到你那里来，
如那夕阳的余光，
映在沉默的星天的边上。

Let my thoughts come to you,

when I am gone,

like the after glow of sunset

at the margin of starry silence.

在我的心头燃点起那
休憩的黄昏星吧，
然后让黑夜向我微语着爱情。

Light in my heart

the evening star of rest

and then let the night whisper to me of love.

我是一个在黑暗中的孩子。

我从夜的被单里向您伸出我的双手，

母亲。

I am a child in the dark.

I stretch my hands through the coverlet of night for thee,

Mother.

275.

白天的工作完了。
把我的脸掩藏在您的臂间吧，
母亲。
让我入梦吧。

The day of work is done.

Hide my face in your arms,

Mother.

Let me dream.

集会时的灯光，
点了很久，
会散时，
灯便立刻灭了。

The lamp of meeting

burns long;

it goes out in a moment

at the parting.

当我死时，
世界呀，
请在你的沉默中，
替我留着"我已经爱过了"这句话吧。

One word keep for me in thy silence,

O World,

when I am dead,

"I have loved."

我们

在热爱世界时

便生活在这世界上。

We

live in this world

when we love it.

让死者
有那不朽的名，
但让生者
有那不朽的爱。

Let the dead

have the immortality of fame,

but the living

the immortality of love.

我看见你，
像那半醒的婴孩在黎明的微光里看见他的母亲，
于是微笑而又睡去了。

I have seen thee

as the half-awakened child sees his mother in the dusk of the dawn

and then smiles and sleeps again.

281·

我将死了又死，
以明白
生是无穷无尽的。

I shall die again and again

to know that

life is inexhaustible.

当我和拥挤的人群一同在路上走过时，
我看见您从阳台上送过来的微笑，
我歌唱着，
忘却了所有的喧哗。

While I was passing with the crowd in the road

I saw thy smile from the balcony

and I sang

and forgot all noise.

283.

爱就是
充实了的生命，
正如盛满了酒的酒杯。

Love

is life in its fullness

like the cup with its wine.

他们点了他们自己的灯，
在他们的寺院内，
吟唱他们自己的话语。

但是小鸟们却在你的晨光中，
唱着你的名字，
——因为你的名字便是快乐。

They light their own lamps

and sing their own words

in their temples.

But the birds sing thy name

in thine own morning light,

—for thy name is joy.

285.

领我
到您的沉寂的中心，
使我的心充满了歌吧。

Lead me

in the centre of thy silence

to fill my heart with songs.

让那些选择了他们自己的焰火咝咝的世界的人，
就生活在那里吧。
我的心渴望着您的繁星，
我的上帝。

Let them live

who choose in their own hissing world of fireworks.

My heart longs for thy stars,

my God.

爱的痛苦环绕着我的一生，
像汹涌的大海似的唱着；
而爱的快乐却像鸟儿们在花林里似的唱着。

Love's pain sang round my life

like the unplumbed sea,

and love's joy sang like birds in its flowering groves.

假如您愿意，
您就熄了灯吧。
我将明白您的黑暗，
而且将喜爱它。

Put out the lamp
when thou wishest.
I shall know thy darkness
and shall love it.

289.

当我在那日子的终了，
站在您的面前时，
您将看见我的伤疤，
而知道我有我的许多创伤，
但也有我的医治的法儿。

When I stand before thee
at the day's end
thou shalt see my scars
and know that I had my wounds
and also my healing.

总有一天，
我要在别的世界的晨光里对你唱道：
"我以前在地球的光里，
在人的爱里，
已经见过你了。"

Some day

I shall sing to thee in the sunrise of some other world,

"I have seen thee

before in the light of the earth,

 in the love of man."

从别的日子里飘浮到我的生命里的云，
不再落下雨点或引起风暴了，
却只给予我的夕阳的天空以色彩。

Clouds come floating into my life from other days

no longer to shed rain or usher storm

but to give colour to my sunset sky.

真理

引起了反对它自己的狂风骤雨，

那场风雨吹散了真理的广播的种子。

Truth

raises against itself the storm

that scatters its seeds broadcast.

昨夜的风雨
给今日的早晨
戴上了金色的和平。

The storm of the last night

has crowned this morning

with golden peace.

真理
仿佛带了它的结论而来；
而那结论
却产生了它的第二个。

Truth

seems to come with its final word;

and the final word

gives birth to its next.

他是有福的，
因为他的名望
并没有比他的真实更光亮。

Blessed is he

whose fame

does not outshine his truth.

您的名字的甜蜜充溢着我的心，
而我忘掉了我自己的
——就像您的早晨的太阳升起时，
那大雾便消失了。

Sweetness of thy name fills my heart

when I forget mine

—like thy morning sun

when the mist is melted.

上帝在我的黄昏的微光中，
带着花到我这里来。
这些花都是我过去的，
在他的花篮中还保存得很新鲜。

God comes to me in the dusk of my evening

with the flowers

from my past

kept fresh in his basket.

图书在版编目（CIP）数据

飞鸟集：泰戈尔作品集：中英对照彩绘珍藏版 / （印）
泰戈尔著；郑振铎译 . — 北京：化学工业出版社，2016.8
（2024.5 重印）
ISBN 978-7-122-27298-0

Ⅰ . ①飞… Ⅱ . ①泰… ②郑… Ⅲ . ①英语－汉语－对照
读物②诗集－印度－现代 Ⅳ . ① H319.4：I

中国版本图书馆 CIP 数据核字 (2016) 第 126520 号

责任编辑：马　骄　梁郁菲　　　　　封面设计：尹琳琳
责任校对：王素芹　　　　　　　　　内文设计：今亮后声 HOPESOUND
pankouyuya@163.com

出版发行：化学工业出版社（北京市东城区青年湖南街 13 号　邮政编码 100011）
印　　装：北京建宏印刷有限公司
880mm×1230mm 1/32　印张 10　字数 200 千字　2024 年 5 月北京第 1 版第 2 次印刷

购书咨询：010-64518888　　　　　售后服务：010-64518899
网　　址：http://www.cip.com.cn
凡购买本书，如有缺损质量问题，本社销售中心负责调换。

定　价：58.00 元